This is

Buenos Aires

de Dios
EDITORES

This is Buenos Aires
Copyright © 2006
de Dios Editores
Buenos Aires / Argentina

Concept: Julián de Dios
Edition: Guillermina Gómez Romero
Translation: Nicholas Tozer & Ruth Muchnik
Research: Gabriel Magda y Soledad Acuña
Art: Micaela Frei
Legal Affairs: Ignacio de las Carreras / www.demarcas.com

de Dios Editores
info@dediosonline.com
www.dediosonline.com

This is Buenos Aires.
ISBN 10: 987-9445-50-3
ISBN 13: 978-987-9445-50-1
First Edition - October 2006
Printed in Buenos Aires - Argentina
3.000 copies printed in Cuatro Colores

Special Sales: For special copies, translations or wholesale purchases, contact to: cdelia@dediosonline.com

Photographs: Julián de Dios

Other photographs:
Julia de Dios: 51a.
Eduardo Longoni: 11a.
Guillermina Gómez Romero: 36a, 36b, 84a, 84b, 84c, 85a, 85b, 85c, 88f, 91d, 93e.
Maximiliano Vaccaro: 46b.
Melito Cerezo / Asociación Argentina de Polo: 87a.
Subsecretaría de Turismo de la Ciudad Autónoma de Buenos Aires: 3a, 10a, 10b, 12a, 12b, 20a, 24a, 45b, 48a, 48c, 49a, 52a, 54b, 73a, 74c, 80a, 81a. Fotos cedidas por la Subsecretaría de Turismo de la Ciudad de Buenos Aires - www.bue.gov.ar
Gentileza Revista Gente, Editorial Atlántida: 4c.
Teatro Colón: 53a, 53b, 53c.
Archivo Histórico de la Nación: 4a.
Museo Eva Perón: 4b, 71a, 71b, 71c.
Casino de Buenos Aires: 21b.
Esquina Carlos Gardel: 48b.

de Dios, Julián
    This is Buenos Aires - 1a ed. - Buenos Aires : de Dios Editores, 2005.
    96 p.; 26x20 cm. Traducido por: Nicholas Tozer
    ISBN 987-9445-50-3
    1. Turismo-Buenos Aires. I. Tozer, Nicholas, trad. II. Título
    CDD 338.479 109 821 1

9 de Julio Avenue. *With a length of three kilometers, it is famous for being the world's widest avenue.*

Buenos Aires in a few words

With a surface of 202 sq. km Buenos Aires, the capital of Argentina, is the largest city of the country and one of the most important in South America. Its boundaries are the Río de la Plata to the East, the Riachuelo to the South and the Avenida Circunvalación General Paz ring road in the North and West. Its population is about three million inhabitants in the Metropolitan area and 10 millions if including the Greater Buenos Aires area, a figure that makes it one of the 10 most populated cities on the planet. **"The Queen of the River Plate"** gained its nickname thanks to the cultural diversity conveyed by the immigrants who arrived between the late 19th and the early 20th Centuries. Thousands of Italian, Spanish, French, British and German people, among other nationalities and creeds who were fleeing from wars and crisis, found shelter in these lands. Back then, Buenos Aires was the entrance door for these hope-loaded ships. As a result, Buenos Aires is the most European city of Latin America, a combination of Italian buildings, French parks, large Spanish houses that, together with the magic of tango, turned it into one of the world's most sophisticated metropolis. From the elegance of the neighborhoods of Recoleta and Plaza San Martín, with its French buildings, to the picturesque neighborhood of La Boca, as well as the historical center of the city with its well-known Plaza de Mayo surrounded by the Cathedral, the Cabildo and Government House, among other old buildings. Without neglecting Palermo with all its facets, from the traditional woods, the Zoo and the Botanical Gardens that constitute the green lung of the city, up to the old Palermo Viejo, -the neighborhood J. L. Borges once walked through that is now a trendy district- also known as Palermo Soho and Palermo Hollywood. Puerto Madero lies by the waters of the river, with state-of-the-art buildings and hotels sharing their space with the old red-brick dock warehouses that now house restaurants, stores and offices. All this is Buenos Aires, a metropolis to visit and get to know step by step.

History

The Querandí Indians were the inhabitants of Buenos Aires when, in 1536, the Spanish settler Pedro de Mendoza founded the city under the name of Ciudad de Nuestra Señora del Buen Ayre. The hostility of indigenous people forced the Spaniards to leave only to return fifty years later in order to proceed with the final foundation of the city. Juan de Garay founded the second settlement in 1580 naming it Santísima Trinidad and Puerto Santa María de los Buenos Aires' or Holy Trinity and Port of St. Mary of the Good Winds. The settlement slowly began growing around the main Plaza Mayor square, surrounded by the vast fields that were thought to be infinite. Around the 18th Century, the city was already inhabited by twenty thousand souls. At the end of the same century, it became the capital of the Viceroyalty of the River Plate comprising Argentina, Bolivia, Paraguay and Uruguay. The first populated neighborhoods were San Telmo and Montserrat, both lying on the shores of the River Plate. It is in this area of the city where the visitor can trace the origins of the city, in places such as the Lezama Park or the Manzana de las Luces. In 1806 and 1807, Buenos Aires underwent an invasion by English troops that were expelled by an incipient popular militia. This heroic deed encouraged the local inhabitants and on May 25, 1810, an Open Assembly was held. As a result Viceroy Cisneros was ousted and a new Government Junta presided over by Cornelio Saavedra, was appointed. In 1824, Bernardino Rivadavia took office as President of Argentina and in 1853, the Argentine National Constitution was proclaimed, laying the foundations for the present-day Argentina. In the 19th Century, the port of Buenos Aires was the point of arrival for the great immigration current promoted by the Argentine State in order to populate the country. The Argentine population increased from ninety thousand people in 1854 to six hundred and seventy thousand in 1895. In the early 20th Century, Buenos Aires was already the most populated city of the whole of Latin America, with over one million inhabitants. Since then, it has preserved this open spirit that has made it into one of the most important cities of the world. With a unique personality where the passion for tango, the craftiness of soccer, the elegance of French architecture, the Italian flavours, the Spanish traditions... and more, much more, coexist.

Historical images. *The Graf Zeppelin flying over the city, a demonstration in Plaza de Mayo and J.L. Borges in San Telmo.*

Porteño details. *The colors of La Boca, the Obelisk from an unusual perspective, the 'adoquin' cobble-stones, Gardel's smile...*

Description

The Argentine Capital consists of 47 neighborhoods characterized by their autonomy from the national and provincial governments, under the leadership of the Head of Government of the City of Buenos Aires. At first glance, the **"Queen of the River Plate"** overwhelms even the most experienced visitor: the width of the Avenida 9 de Julio, the conglomeration of buildings, the overpopulated streets, the car horns, everything contributes to a sense of chaos. However, you start falling in love with her as you get to know her. Its layout is simple; its streets run from East to West and North to South. The neuralgic point is located at the Cid Campeador Monument, where the neighborhood of Caballito begins.

For transportation the city has five subway lines that converge downtown and cover the different neighborhoods.

Over 140 bus lines carry passengers to the furthest places of the city, including the Greater Buenos Aires. Besides, there are 39 thousand taxicabs, which make it one of the cities with greater percentage of taxis per inhabitant.

The climate provides an annual average temperature of 18° C. The best seasons to visit it are fall and spring, with average temperatures that allow you to walk. Winter, especially July and August, are cold months, therefore, you must definitely wear a coat and a scarf, while January and February are very hot, ideal to get to know the nocturnal Buenos Aires, that of tiny tables in the street and friendly chatting, accompanied by a cold beer.

The countless nationalities inhabiting the city have brought with them a broad spectrum as far as gastronomy is concerned: there are restaurants that belong to the most varied ethnicities, although most visitors arrive in search for the traditional 'asado criollo' (creole barbecue), that can be enjoyed in different 'parrilla' grill restaurants of the city.

The cultural and entertainment supply of Buenos Aires is another remarkable characteristic of this metropolis. Buenos Aires offers well-known museums, cultural centers, art galleries as well as a full billboard offering a broad variety of theater shows in the main venues of Avenida Corrientes and also in the off-Corrientes circuit, spread throughout different neighborhoods of the city.

President Avellaneda Bridge. *Inaugurated in 1908, it worked as a ferry. Today, it is the symbol of the Vuelta de Rocha.*

La Boca Republic. *In the 19th Century a group of genovese immigrants tried to set up the independent Republic of La Boca.*

The Neighborhood of La Boca

According to tradition, La Boca used to be a typical Italian immigrant neighborhood, something proved by the countless "cantina" restaurants offering typical dishes of the peninsula that are certainly worth tasting. **Caminito,** the pedestrian street, is perhaps the most famous postcard of Buenos Aires. It is a hot-spot to enjoy spontaneous shows and varied handicrafts among highly colorful corrugated sheet-coated houses, chords of Tango and street performers showing their skills. La Boca also offers an appealing cultural activity: the **La Boca Fine Arts Museum**, a building donated by Benito Quinquela Martín -the great painter who best portrayed the life in the old port- is now assembled. On the other hand, the **Proa Foundation** organizes exhibitions by contemporary *avant-garde* artists' and its terrace offers a tempting invitation to witness the sunset over the river. Another attraction is the old **President Avellaneda moving bridge**, dating from 1908. A newer bridge, from 1940, is right beside it. A visit to the neighborhood would be incomplete if you fail to visit the **Boca Juniors Athletic Club**, where Diego Maradona played soccer. You can visit the stadium, known as "La Bombonera" (The Chocolate Box) and the "Boca Passion Museum".

Caminito. One of the most representative postcards of Buenos Aires. A 'must' visit, ideal for the weekends. Flanked by houses painted in brilliant colors and populated by street artists, it was the stage of a great part of the neighborhood's history.

Picturesque. *The neighborhood of La Boca is a fun tour by nature, from the sheet metal clad houses painted with vibrant colors to the works of the artisans who lean out of the balconies, the old iron fences, the typical characters...*

A pause to enjoy. *To appreciate the rhythm of Caminito, nothing is better than sitting down to have a delicious cup of coffee or a beer at one of the old bars bordering the Riachuelo and become a witness of the movement of the neighborhood.*

Boca Juniors. *According to popular legend, the blue and gold color club is supported by half the Argentine population plus one.*

River Plate. *Another great club of the Argentine Soccer League. With Boca Juniors they clash in the most vibrant game of the soccer tournament. The club has a breathtaking stadium known as "the Monumental" in the Núñez area, one of the most elegant neighborhoods.*

The "hincha" soccer fans. *The love for their favorite club can be seen in the outfits, the faces, the flags and in the songs ...*

Boca vs. River: a passion

Soccer is the most popular sport of Argentina and the "classic" local derby game between Boca Juniors and River Plate is the most important duel of the year. According to the English newspaper 'The Guardian', attending the football game between these two teams at the "La Bombonera" is the most intense sports experience of the world. During the game, the fans unfold all their colorfulness: T-shirts, hats, flags, all kinds of makeup, color-flares ... outside the stadium. The city comes to a halt and people gather at friends' houses or cafés in order to watch the game on TV or listen to it on the radio. Every "porteño" (inhabitant of the 'port', that is, Buenos Aires) is a soccer team fan, a love that remains unchanged no matter what. According to the legend, "half the Argentineans plus one are Boca fans", the club where Diego Maradona played and wore the number 10 shirt. Beyond statistics, Boca Juniors, River Plate, Independiente, Racing Club, San Lorenzo de Almagro and Vélez Sarsfield are some of the most popular soccer-team clubs in Buenos Aires.

Details. *A stroll around the San Telmo area means paying attention to both the small and big details so as to recognize the spirit of one of the oldest neighborhoods of Buenos Aires.*

San Telmo

In San Telmo you breath the history. It is the neighborhood that shows the deepest roots of Buenos Aires, a fact that can be easily appreciated in its low-house architecture, narrow fronts and iron railings. The **Lezama Park**, where the first foundation of the city took place in 1536, is located here as well as the **Historical Museum**, with over 40 thousand pieces that tell us the history of Argentina, including San Martín's sword. The religious roots of the city can also be felt in this neighborhood, the **Church of San Ignacio,** the oldest of Buenos Aires and the breathtaking **Basílica of Santo Domingo**, with Belgrano's Mausoleum, among others. The enchantment of history continues with the **Manzana de las Luces**, a series of buildings dating from the mid 17th Century constructed by the Jesuits, that include underground tunnels. The **Modern Arts Museum**, an old tobacco warehouse where a remarkable collection of modern art is exhibited with masterpieces by Picasso, Kandinsky, Matisse, Berni and Pettoruti is close to the Lezama Park. San Telmo also offers a vast gastronomic variety, from large popular restaurants known as 'bodegones' with low-priced generous dishes to remarkable 'parrilla' grills, famous restaurants and countless bars with a young and trendy atmosphere. Do not miss the historical cafés around Plaza Dorrego, a 'must' stop for any visitor as well as the tango district along Balcarce St., with a broad scope of tango shows that often comprise music and dancing with dinner included.

Dorrego Square Antiques Fair. *Each weekend, the old 'plaza' turns into the stage for a thrilling fair, where real treasures can be found.*

Corners with history. *San Telmo houses some of the historical cafés that have remained unchanged for decades.*

Tango. *During the weekends, the spontaneous 'milonga' dances are a tradition that is carried out together with the antiques fair and get as crowded as Dorrego Square itself.*

In the rhythm of the 2x4. *The streets surrounding Dorrego Square are another stage chosen by tango groups.*

A postcard from early last century. *In the San Telmo area, motorcades of old cars are organized several times a year, allowing them to crisscross the area once again, to the applause of the onlookers and surprise of young people.*

Granaderos Band in Dorrego Square. *The old San Telmo square is the stage for various historic commemorations.*

Plaza Dorrego

Visiting Plaza Dorrego, in the old neighborhood of San Telmo, is another 'must' of this great city. The Antiques Fair is held here every Sunday, with tens of stands that offer everything from antique coins to stamps, books, crockery, silverware, garments stemming from different ages as well as old records by Gardel.

The nearby streets are also populated with antique shops offering larger objects such as furniture, statues, ancient lamps, century old trunks. The spirit of the fair is complemented by the performance of street dances known as street "milongas".

On sunny days, the surrounding bars offer simple dishes served at their outdoor tables. When it is cold, the historical cafés become the real protagonists: the Plaza Dorrego Bar, at the corner of Defensa St. and Humberto I° St., or the El Federal on Perú St. and Carlos Calvo St., a reminder of how the cafés of the 40's looked and El Hipopótamo, on 401 Brazil St., in Parque Lezama, is ideal to have a coffee while sitting by the window.

Tradition. *On Sundays, the stands occupy the nearby streets.*

Small tables on the sidewalk. *Ideal to enjoy the street show.*

Defensa Street. *Many antiques are exhibited outdoors.*

Folklore. *The music of inland Argentina is also present.*

Tango. *Street 'milonga' to the rhythm of a guitar.*

Buenos Aires at night. *From Puerto Madero, one of the most beautiful panoramic views of the city can be truly appreciated.*

Puerto Madero

This is the youngest neighbourhood of the city. It stretches out from the Southern Coastal Nature Reserve up to the Ingeniero Huergo Ave., at the bottom of the Government House and from Cecilia Grierson Street up to Juan de Garay Ave., south of the city.

The old port of Buenos Aires gave way to one of the most modern districts of the city where the traditional red-brick docks were recycled and turned into condominiums, offices, lofts, trendy restaurants, stores and movie theaters, now located in the Western sector of the Port. Dock 3 is crossed by the famous Puente de la Mujer bridge dedicated to women and created by the spanish architect Santiago Calatrava, with a length of 160 meters it connects with the new sector of the neighborhood. According to its creator the bridge recreates the figure of a woman dancing Tango.

This detail is not just a coincidence since most streets in Puerto Madero are named after famous women. In the waters of the same dock the Presidente Sarmiento frigate is now located, a naval training sailing ship that traveled a distance equivalent to 42 times a round the world. In the meantime, Dock 4 houses in its waters the oldest Argentine ship afloat, the Uruguay corvette, a source of national pride. It is right here that the exclusive Puerto Madero Yacht Club is located.

The physiognomy of the Eastern area of the Port changes and is turned into mirrored buildings, five-star hotels and deluxe apartment towers.

The Costanera T. Achával Rodríguez Ave. separates the city from the Nature Reserve, and a few steps away from there you will see the beautiful Sea Nymphs Fountain, a piece of art by the Argentine sculptor Lola Mora that, at the time, was considered 'immoral'. An interesting collection of real-size replicas of the world's most important sculptures, such as the "Moses" and the "David" by Michelangelo, next to the "Venus of Milo" and the "Victory of Samotracia", among other famous masterpieces, can be found at the Calcos Museum.

Those who miss gambling can visit the Floating Casino in Dock I, a Mississippi-style paddle ship where the only casino in the capital city operates.

Puerto Madero Yacht Club. *Located a stone throw away from downtown; it is one of the most distinguished clubs of Buenos Aires.*

Women's Bridge. *Designed by the prestigious Spanish architect Santiago Calatrava, it represents a woman dancing tango.*

A new district in the old port. *In Puerto Madero, the cranes and other old port equipment can be seen.*

Designs. *The new buildings of Puerto Madero are dazzling because of their design and modernity.*

Port. *The northern area of Puerto Madero is where the terminals that handle both military and cruise vessels are located.*

Floating Casino. *With a style that reminds us of the Mississippi river boats, the Puerto Madero Casino is the first of the city.*

Old docks. *They were recycled respecting their original structure. Inside, they house lofts, offices, restaurants and movie theaters.*

__Activities in Puerto Madero.__ Sailing, running, having something to drink in the bars, participating in travelling exhibitions...

Images by the river. *Cows painted by outstanding artists, a sculpture of Juan M. Fangio, a historical ship...*

XXI Century Buenos Aires. *With the arrival of the new millennium, the city once again paid attention to the Río de la Plata. Modern luxury towers, parks bordering the coast and sporting marinas are some of the most recent urban undertakings.*

Nature Reserve. *An ideal place to breathe pure air, ride a bicycle, run or simply enjoy your free time.*

Another perspective. *From the Nature Reserve, a different panoramic view of downtown Buenos Aires can be appreciated.*

Costanera Sur Ecological Reserve

Opposite to Puerto Madero, lying by the Río de la Plata, is where this 350 hectare Nature Reserve is located. An ideal place to visit that allows you to be in touch with nature and constitutes an unbelievable green lung a stone's throw away from the Obelisk. It has two circuits to enjoy either on bicycle or by foot and the entrance is free. The 3,300 meters long Laguna de los Patos' Circuit, can be accessed through Brazil Street and the 2,200 meters long River Circuit, through Viamonte Street. Both offer unique perspectives of Buenos Aires and its buildings, emerging among pastures and foxtail grass. The flora and fauna of the Reserve is typical of the Pampas and the river Parana Delta. It is visited by 250 bird species every year that vary according to the season and also by mammals such as the otter, the "cuis" guinea pig, the "overo" and red opossums and a great number of reptiles.

Plaza de Mayo. *Ever since the Open Cabildo of 1810, Plaza de Mayo has been the main stage of Argentine political life.*

Plaza de Mayo

From the epic days of May 1810, up to the present, every important event that brings together this society, takes place in the famous square. It is surrounded by historical buildings, and Government House or the Pink House, where the Argentine President governs together with the members of his closest team, comes first. Then, it is also bordered by the Metropolitan Cathedral, where the remains of General José de San Martín rest as well as by the old Spanish colonial Cabildo town hall and the Municipal Palace, seat of the Head of Government of the Autonomous City of Buenos Aires. Plaza de Mayo, as seen today, was redesigned by the French landscape artist Carlos Thays in 1900 but the May Pyramid, located in its center, dates from 1856. The Square is especially meaningful for the Argentineans since both the saddest and most glorious events of their national history took place here. Even now, demonstrations in favor of or against different causes are either started or ended in Plaza de Mayo. For any organizer, whether the President, a trade union or a social movement leader, 'filling the square' means success. One of the best remembered events in popular memory is Eva Peron's last speech from one of the balconies of the Government House.

Historic Cabildo. *The remnants of the original building where the May 1810 Revolution was conceived.*

Casa Rosada. *Seat of the Executive power, where the President of Argentina and his closest assistants work.*

Pyramid of May. *Symbol of the epic of Argentine Independence, it is crowned by a sculpture representing the Republic.*

Julio A. Roca Diagonal. *From the corner with Bolívar Street, some of the most beautiful domes of Buenos Aires can be appreciated.*

Votive flame. Located in front of the Metropolitan Cathedral.

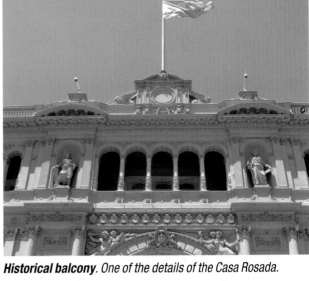
Historical balcony. One of the details of the Casa Rosada.

Symbol. The Mothers of Plaza de Mayo's handkerchief.

Changing of the Guard. Ceremony at Plaza de Mayo.

Flags. Street sellers near Plaza de Mayo.

Christopher Columbus. Detail of the statue devoted to Columbus.

Metropolitan Cathedral. *The Cathedral - construction of which began in 1791 - is located on one side of Plaza de Mayo.*

Metropolitan Cathedral

The Metropolitan Cathedral of the City of Buenos Aires, named after the Holy Trinity, is located in front of the historical Plaza de Mayo, on the corner of Rivadavia and San Martín. It is the sixth temple built as a Cathedral since the arrival of the Spaniards. The first one made of 'adobe' bricks and straw was put up in 1593 and had to be demolished because of its fragile construction. The subsequent temples suffered the same fate, falling down a short time after having been built. The present church building was begun in the 18th Century and finally finished in the early 20th Century. All this accounts for the diversity of its styles, from Baroque to Romanic, due to the many architects

and builders who took part in building it and who changed their minds as the construction was coming to an end. The front is a copy of the Bourbon Palais, with the twelve columns representing the twelve apostles. The eternal votive flame is located by the group of columns, as a tribute to General San Martín and the Unknown Soldier of the war of Argentine Independence.

It has three naves within; the main one is approximately 100 meters long and its dome is 46 meters high, besides its 3,000 sq. meters of floor covered with petite mosaics. Liberator General José de San Martín's Mausoleum, where his remains rest, stands out on the right side. It was declared National Historical Monument in 1942.

Pilar Basílica. *One of the oldest and most beautiful churches of Buenos Aires. It was built during the first half of the 18th Century.*

Historical Churches

Some of the Churches and Convents that remain erect in different neighborhoods of Buenos Aires are as old as the tunnels.

The oldest of them all is the **San Ignacio de Loyola Church**, inaugurated in 1722 at the corner of Bolívar and Alsina, right in the heart of the Montserrat neighborhood. The **Nuestra Señora del Pilar Basílica** located in the neighborhood of Recoleta by the cemetery and dates from 1732. The baroque **Santa Catalina de Siena Church**, with its impressive colonial patio, is located on San Martín and Viamonte St., in the neighborhood of San Nicolás, and dates from 1700. Equally old is the **Nuestra Señora de la Merced Basílica** on Reconquista St., in downtown Buenos Aires, with a pleasant garden that can be visited. The **San Pedro González Telmo Church**, built in 1806, is located in San Telmo as well as the breathtaking **Santo Domingo Convent**, on the corner of Belgrano Ave. and Defensa, corresponding to the late 18th Century, where the mausoleum of General Manuel Belgrano, one of the heroes of the Argentine Independence, is located.

San Roque. *Historical chapel of the neighborhood of Montserrat.*

Santo Domingo. *Designated as a National Historic Monument.*

San Pedro Telmo. *A few meters away from Dorrego Square.*

San Ignacio. *An example of Jesuit baroque architecture.*

Zanjón de Granados. A trip to the colonial past of Buenos Aires via a tour through the underground tunnels.

Tunnels in the city

The mysterious tunnels of Buenos Aires were built during the colonial era and used to connect the main buildings surrounding the main 'Plaza Mayor' square, that is, the present Plaza de Mayo. There are several places that organize guided tours, allowing you to walk through the guts of the city. One of the most interesting guided tours is the one offered by the '**Zanjón de Granados'**, with tunnels that followed a natural water course that flowed into the Río de la Plata. Some historians place the first foundation of Buenos Aires at this site. Remains of old foundation walls, floors and wells built between 1730 and 1865 can be seen here. Also the tunnels of the '**Manzana de las Luces**' around Bolívar, Moreno, Alsina and Peru Streets - whose name, block of lights, was due to the fact that during the 19th Century it used to be the intellectual center of the city as well as those of the **Taylor Customs**, near Government House.

Manzana de las Luces. Historical tunnels of Buenos Aires.

Buenos Aires Domes

Buenos Aires is a city that forces you to pay attention to heights, never ceasing to look up, especially in neighborhoods such as Montserrat and Congreso. It is on Av. de Mayo where the dome of the old **La Prensa Newspaper** (Av. de Mayo 575) stands out, with a bronze female figure holding a torch and a sheet of paper, symbolizing freedom of speech. The **Urquiza Anchorena Palace** (Av. de Mayo 747), built in 1921, has another of the remarkable domes of the city. The dome of the **Barolo Palace** (Av. de Mayo 1370) is one of the most attractive ones; the building was inaugurated in 1923 and its dome, at the height of a 24th floor, was the highest of the city until the Kavanagh building was put up in 1935. A few meters away, you can find the famous red domes of the **Edificio La Inmobiliaria**, on Av. de Mayo between Luis Sáenz Peña and San José, belonging to the NeoRenaissance period and on whose top floor the Venus and Apollo statues can be made out. At the corner of the Avenues Callao and Rivadavia is where the Art Nouveau domes of **El Molino Cafeteria** can be seen. It was designed and built in 1905 by the italian Francesco Gianotti. Countless other domes crown the buildings in the city, such as that of the **Naval Centre**, on the corner of Florida and Av. Córdoba; that of the **Customs** building on Azopardo and Paseo Colón; the other one belonging to the **Government of the City**, at Bolívar and Rivadavia and also the dome of the **Bartolome Mitre Railway Station**, in Retiro.

In the heights. From the replica of a windmill to a dome devoted to Dante Alighieri.

Corners. *At the beginning of the past century, Avenida de Mayo used to be a meeting point, with historical cafés that can still be visited.*

Avenida de Mayo

It was inaugurated in 1885. To be built, artists from many different nationalities were convened, and they are responsible for the facades of the buildings. However, it is the most Spanish artery of Buenos Aires. Avenida de Mayo is a one-kilometer long stroll that allows you to enjoy an exquisite architecture while obliging you to look up high at the wonderful domes that crown many of the buildings. Once Argentine Presidents have been sworn in, they go along this avenue all the way from the Congress to Government House. From Plaza de Mayo to the Dos Congresos Square, the following buildings stand out: the colonial **Cabildo**, dating from 1765, where the May Revolution was conceived; the **Municipal Palace**, from the early 20th Century, whose style is Academic French; the old **La Prensa Newspaper** building, that is presently housing the City Culture Secretariat, dating from the late 19th Century and whose dome is crowned by a 3000 kilo bronze lamplight and an allegoric statue, with journalism represented by a woman. The **Tortoni Café**, inaugurated in 1858, was famous because of the meetings held there by prestigious personalities. The historical **Castelar Hotel**, a meeting point for politicians and writers as well as temporary home of the Spanish poet Federico García Lorca. The **Teatro Avenida**, re-opened in 1994 with a performance by opera singer Plácido Domingo.

The **Barolo Palace**, one of the most dazzling buildings of the tour by the Italian architect Mario Palanti in an expressionist style, was inaugurated in 1922 and well deserves special reference. It is in **Plaza de los Dos Congresos** where you can find a masterpiece by Auguste Rodin: **"The Thinker"**, one of the six authenticated copies of this sculpture spread around the globe. The visit finishes at the **Argentine National Congress**, a Greco-Roman building from the early 20th Century, with an amazing 30 thousand ton dome and beautiful inner rooms.

Avenida de Mayo. *It was inaugurated in the late 19th Century, commemorating the Centenary of the May Revolution.*

Café Tortoni. *Its tables witnessed the presence of Borges, Pirandello and García Lorca, among other personalities.*

The 36 Billiards*. On Avenida de Mayo, it was the first 'porteño' café with a room especially devoted to billiards.*

Plaza Dorrego Bar. *A classic of San Telmo. A 'must' once you have visited the Antiques Fair of the neighboring square.*

Cafés of Buenos Aires

The cafés of Buenos Aires are the stages for rituals as "porteño" as tango: meet friends for a cup of coffee, flip through a newspaper, sit by the window to watch people walk by, write a love letter... In the city there as many bars as histories, and some of them have been designated architectural heritage of Buenos Aires. Some of those that cannot be missed are the historic **Tortoni**, on Avenida de Mayo where Jorge Luis Borges was frequently to be seen; **Los 36 billares**, famous as the birthplace of the most famous billiards' players, the **Bar Dorrego** by the little square in San Telmo; and the **Café Homero Manzi**, in Boedo, chosen by the tangophiles...

A 'porteño' ceremony. *Sitting at a table to watch people passing by.*

Plaza de los Dos Congresos. "Kilometer Zero" is located here.

The Thinker. One of the six replicas of A. Rodin's masterpiece.

Congress Palace

This breathtaking Greco-Roman Palace is the seat of the Legislative Power, where the Lower House of Representatives and the Senate operate. It was built between 1898 and 1908 and was designed by the Italian architect Víctor Meano, who was inspired by the American Capitol in Washington. Its 30 thousand ton dome is one of the most beautiful in the country, and is 80 meters wide and copper coated. In order to be supported by the building, it was built above a ten meter deep foundation with an inverted dome.

The main entrance known as the 'Entrada de Honor' is located on Entre Rios Ave. and is used for ceremonial purposes. Standing out over this entrance is the famous 'quadriga' sculpture; an eight-meter high work-of-art made out of bronze that weighs over 20 tons by sculptor Victor de Pol. The chariot drawn by four horses abreast symbolizes the triumphant Republic, led by the winged Victory. Inside, the most luxurious rooms are the House of Representatives chamber, the Lost Steps Hall and the Blue Room. On Argentine national holidays, the lights on the buildings dome are lit enhancing its beauty even further.

Panoramic view from Palacio Barolo. *The Plaza de los Dos Congresos was designed by Carlos Thays in 1909.*

Congress Palace*. Seat of the Legislative Power. It was inaugurated in 1906, taking Washington's Capitol Hill as its model.*

'Porteño filete' paintwork. *Houses on Jean Jaures Street, near the old Abasto Market, ornamented with 'porteño filete' paintwork.*

Street tributes. *On Zelaya side road, a series of murals devoted to the 'Creole Thrush' Carlos Gardel, have been painted.*

Abasto Market. *The old fruit and vegetable market was transformed into the city's biggest shopping mall.*

Abasto

The Abasto is a synonym of Gardel.

This neighbourhood, lying off Corrientes Avenue, is where the most famous tango singer of history, Carlos Gardel, known as the "Creole thrush", lived and spent most of his life. The "B" line subway station and a local street have both been given his name, as well as a statue before which everyone can take that 'picture to remember'. At the corner of Carlos Gardel and Tomás de Anchorena streets is where the **"La Esquina de Carlos Gardel",** a restaurant that offers a dazzling first-class tango dinner-show is located. The epicentre of the neighbourhood is, undoubtedly, the Abasto Shopping mall, located in the same place where the old Abasto Fruit and Vegetable Market, which used to supply most of the city, was located.

Now fully recycled, it is at present the largest shopping mall of the city, with over 230 clothing, shoe, book and toy stores as well as various movie theatres where non-commercial movies are screened. The third floor houses the **Children's Museum**, a children's custom-made city where they can play while pretending to be bankers, cooks, bricklayers, plumbers, among many other crafts. The mall also has a food patio as well as an electronic games area aimed at children of all ages. Recently, several hotels of different categories have opened their doors along Corrientes Avenue, proving that the Abasto area is constantly increasing its tourism appeal.

Carlos Gardel

Together with Diego Maradona, Ernesto "Che" Guevara and María Eva Duarte de Perón, better-known as Evita, he is, undoubtedly, one of the most popular idols of Argentina. One of the best places to recreate the history of the tango singer known as the "creole thrush" is the Carlos Gardel Museum House in the neighborhood of Abasto, at 735 Jean Jaures Street. The singer lived in this typical eight-meter-front "casa chorizo" house together with his mother, from 1927 to 1933, when she decided to return to France. There are souvenirs, photographs and various documents that enable us to imagine Gardel's life. A few steps away from there, along the short Zelaya St., there are various walls with murals dedicated to the singer, a tribute that spreads all over the Abasto neighborhood.

His tomb can be visited at the Chacarita Cemetery -he died in 1935 in an air-crash in Medellín, Colombia. Since then, his figure has continued to grow bigger and bigger over time. A statue here remembers him standing in typical pose, with his eternal smile and dressed in his classical 'Gardelian' clothes and is always decked with fresh flowers. Every June 24, that is, on the day of the anniversary of his death, both singers and fans visit this site in order to pay tribute to him with their songs. It is surprising to see the great amount of plaques that fill the walls of the mausoleum, either paying homage to or thanking him. Since February 6, 1936, the date on which his crowded burial ceremony took place, these have never ceased increasing.

June 24. On the day of his death, his fans gather at his mausoleum.

Gardel Station. Old mural located in the Abasto subway station.

Gardel's Statue. *Work by the sculptor Mariano Pages.*

Chacarita. *The mausoleum in his memory.*

Popular art. *Another mural dedicated to Carlos Gardel.*

Gardel Museum. *The house he lived in now turned into a museum.*

A smell of tango. *In Buenos Aires, there is always an opportunity to dance tango.*

Tango

It was born in the second half of the 19th century in the port of Buenos Aires, in neighborhoods such as La Boca, San Telmo, Montserrat and Pompeya. From there, it was spread throughout the city and, with the voice of Carlos Gardel, it was launched around the world, especially with "Caminito". From its very beginnings, tango showed its changeable profile: first it was simply music played on piano in houses of dubious reputation. Later it was joined by the guitar, the flute and the violin as it started to be accepted in the more prestigious ball-rooms. It was danced among 'porteño' men, the 'arrabaleros', 'guapos', 'malevos' and 'compadritos' of Buenos Aires dressed in their impeccable suits, with shinny shoes and greasy hair-styles. The great change in tango was brought about by the arrival of the 'bandoneon' squeeze box from Germany, an instrument which was to become emblematic of tango and played by great musicians such as Astor Piazzolla. Tango is such a wide ranging rhythm that it can only be compared with Jazz, insofar as its richness and ability to adapt to changing times. But because tango is danced and most forms of popular music are not, it invariably ended up in the concert halls instead of on the streets. In Buenos Aires, you can breathe tango at every corner, and there are countless tango-shows, many including dinner, first-class orchestras, musicals and also 'milonga' dances where you are taught the ABCs of this passionate rhythm. Tango is a synonym of Buenos Aires.

Milongas. *At the Confitería Ideal, is where one of the most genuine 'milonga' dances of Buenos Aires operates.*

Corrientes Avenue and the Obelisk

The Obelisk, one of the classic postcards of the city, is located at the intersection of Avenues Corrientes and 9 de Julio, the most famous corner of Buenos Aires and one of the most photographed spots of Argentina.

At night, Corrientes Ave. becomes the 'Buenos Aires Broadway' with its neon lights announcing the theater plays and musicals that are presently on stage. It is here where most theaters are concentrated, both the traditional and the *avant-garde* type, with performances held Tuesdays through Sundays. This busy avenue, also known as 'the avenue that never sleeps,' is famous for its bookstores with a bohemian atmosphere that have 'infected' the nearby cafés. Some of the most famous cafés are: the La Paz Café, on the corner of Corrientes and Montevideo and the La Giralda Café, at Corrientes and Paraná, very popular because of its chocolate with 'churro' pastries.

The restaurants of the area are part of the history of the city, from the German Zum Edelweiss, where many actors meet after their performances, to the Los Inmortales pizzeria, on whose walls you can admire pictures from the golden age of tango, with Carlos Gardel or Anibal Troilo; the traditional Pippo on Montevideo St., whose good credit rests on its 'vermichelli' pasta with 'tuco and pesto' sauce or any of the nearby pizzerias such as Güerrin or Las Cuartetas that, anything but luxurious, offer abundant portions and on-the-tap beer at any time of the day or night.

'Porteño' Broadway. *Corrientes Avenue is famous for its numerous theaters.*

The Avenue that never sleeps. *An ideal tour for night lovers.*

Symbol of the city. *The Obelisk was put up to commemorate the 4th Centenary of the first foundation of the city.*

Colon Theater. Arturo Toscanini, María Callas, Plácido Domingo, Luciano Pavarotti, Enrico Caruso, performed here...

Colon Theater

It is internationally well-known as one of the lyrical theaters with best acoustics in the world, together with the Scala of Milan. It was inaugurated in 1908 with a performance of the opera 'Aida' by Verdi. Throughout its years of life prestigious artists such as Toscanini, María Callas, Pavarotti, Nijinsky and many other noted stars from all over the globe have performed on its stage. It is not only worth attending an opera or a concert in order to grasp all the splendor of its main auditorium, but also by taking any of the highly interesting guided tours offered daily in various languages, in order to get to know the backstage of this prestigious theater. It has three underground floors that run beneath the 9 de Julio Ave. and where there is a tailor's store with over 80 thousand outfits from different periods, a shoe department with over 20 thousand pairs of shoes, a hairdresser's with its 36 thousand wigs and many other workshops such as a carpentry, where each item that is to be taken on stage, is made by hand. Beyond the backstage tour, there is some data that let us envisage the magnitude of the theater. The main hall has a capacity of 2,500 people; the front stage is 35 meters wide and has a 20 meter diameter rotary platform in its middle. Equally overwhelming is the dome, painted by Raul Soldi, the Argentine painter, covering a surface of 318 sq. meters, from whose center hangs a 700 light bulb crystal chandelier with a diameter of over seven meters. One of the peculiarities of the Colon Theater are the old "*baignoire*" pit boxes of the main auditorium.

Dazzling. *The main auditorium of the theater has a capacity of 2,500 people and a stage with a rotating platform.*

Dome. *The dome of the main auditorium was decorated by the artist Raul Soldi.*

Salón Dorado. *For chamber works.*

Myth & art. *Spontaneous paintings often pay tribute to popular idols such as Ernesto "Che" Guevara.*

Tango. *A mural in Barracas neighborhood.*

Protest. *A favorite subject for graffiti.*

Existentialism. *Art that brings about thought.*

Graffiti of Buenos Aires

Like every great city, Buenos Aires has its graffiti, drawings, popular expressions and notable phrases painted on the walls of vacant lots, the facades of abandoned houses and even on trains, advertising hoardings and buildings. Graffiti artists are painters who have their own style, generally painting with spray and stencil paints, and they rarely do so on request. They can recreate a landscape, an abstract drawing, a portrait or the main popular myths thus ornamenting the different corners of the city. One of the most graffiti-populated areas is Goyeneche Ave. (ex Donado) in the neighborhood of Saavedra. However, this popular art form has been spread throughout the neighborhoods of the city. One of the most flashy graffiti to be seen is the one located on the corner of Avenida de Mayo and B. de Irigoyen Avenues, which represents a typical 'porteño' street scene. As an art form graffiti has an expiration date, since one artist may consider that his own initiative is better and cover a previous work with a new piece of art.

Public art*. On the corner of Avenida de Mayo and Bernardo de Irigoyen, a mural that portrays a typical Buenos Aires scene.*

Florida

The most emblematic pedestrian street of Buenos Aires. It begins at Avenida de Mayo and crosses the Buenos Aires downtown up to Plaza San Martín. A little more than 10 city blocks with all kinds of stores selling everything from jewels, leather clothes, shoes, electronic devices, perfumes, records (CDs and DVDs), books, maps, drugstores, ice cream, cafés and restaurants.

During the week walking along Florida is a hard task that gets even more complicated at midday, when banks, business and office staff and employees take their lunch break while the hucksters and street artists entertain the public with spontaneous performances. Some of the most remarkable spots of this famous pedestrian street are: the Galerías Pacífico, an elegant shopping mall with renowned clothing brands and frescos by Argentine artists Antonio Berni, Juan Carlos Castagnino and Lino Eneas Spilimbergo among others that make the dome incredibly noticeable, besides a food patio and various movie theaters. Just a few steps away from there, the Borges Cultural Center offers interesting artistic exhibitions at an international level as well as some shows. At the corner of Paraguay and Florida, you will find the Florida Garden, a classic 'porteño' café and meeting point for intellectuals and politicians and then, when you are almost in Plaza San Martin, you will be able to see the underground Ruth Benzacar Art Gallery, one of the most important galleries with *avant-garde* artists' exhibitions.

Pedestrian Florida. *A 'must' visit that is born steps away from Plaza de Mayo.*

Galerías Pacífico. *A shopping mall, famous for its murals, carried out by Antonio Berni, Juan C. Castagnino and Spilimbergo.*

Street Musicians. *One of the typical scenes of Florida Street.*

Santa Catalina Convent. *Beautiful cloister dating from 1745.*

Plaza San Martín

Set over a natural embankment, it is one of the most beautiful and most historical parks of Buenos Aires. Since the arrival of the Spaniards, it has fulfilled different functions, from a slave market and bull ring to the barracks of an artillery unit. At the end of the 19th Century, the area was converted into a park with over 300 trees and ever since, it has become one of the emblematic corners of the city. Around the park, there are several mansions that used to belong to aristocratic families which, at present, are official buildings. The Haedo Palace, at the corner of Santa Fe Ave. and Maipú is nowadays the seat of Argentine National Parks Administration; the Paz Palace houses the Military Circle and the National Arms Museum. The exquisite Anchorena Palace, also well-known as Palacio San Martín, is the seat of the Argentine Foreign Ministry. Another remarkable property is the Kavanagh building, inaugurated in 1936, the first skyscraper of South America. Besides these, an important sculpture dedicated to the Liberator of Argentina, General José de San Martín stands out at one end of the square. At the bottom of the embankment, along Av. del Libertador the Malvinas War Monument is located, with the names of the soldiers who died in this conflict engraved in stone. The English Tower is located exactly opposite; a gift from the local British community to Argentina in the rooms of which art exhibitions are held, and with a watchtower on the 6th floor that offers a panoramic view of San Martín Square.

Torre de los Ingleses. *A gift from the British community to Argentina.*

Homage. *Monument dedicated to the fallen during the South Atlantic War.*

San Martín Square. *Set on a beautiful natural embankment, it was here that Buenos Aires' only bullfighting ring was located.*

MNBA. *The country's most important collection of works of art.*

Fernández Blanco Museum. *Valuable heritage of colonial art.*

Decorative Art Museum. *It is located at the Errázuriz Palace.*

Modern Art Museum. *Works by Picasso, Matisse, Berni...*

MALBA. *Private collection of Latin American art with works by Kahlo, Rivera, Do Amaral, Torres García, among other artists.*

Buenos Aires Museums

Buenos Aires is also remarkable because of its prestigious museums and works of art. One of the most important is the National Fine Arts Museum whose patrimony is over eleven thousand works and among which you can find a breathtaking Impressionist collection with masterpieces by Manet, Van Gogh, Gauguin and Degas, besides others by Rembrandt, El Greco, Rubens, Goya, Modigliani, Chagall, Klee, Kandinsky and Picasso, among many others. The Argentine masterpieces can be found on the first floor where there are also temporary exhibitions.

The Buenos Aires Latin American Art Museum MALBA is located a few blocks away, with an interesting collection of the most important contemporary Latinamerican artists such as Kahlo, Berni, Lam, Torres García, Botero and Do Amaral, among others. Besides, the modern building offers exhibitions by contemporary artists, a movie theater screening non-commercial films and an attractive café. The National Decorative Art Museum located in the Errázuriz Palace, is the only palatial mansion open to the general public. It has over four thousand exhibits comprising tapestries, crockery and highly valuable paintings, among which it is worth mentioning works by Rodin, El Greco, Sorolla and Fragonard. A beautiful neo colonial mansion houses the Fernández Blanco Museum, famous for its Ibero-American silverware. Another outstanding museum is the Evita Museum, an interesting tour through the life of one of the most controversial personalities of the 20th Century, materialized in a permanent exhibition of photographs, videos, outfits and souvenirs. It also offers other temporary thematic exhibitions that help to understand that period of the Argentine history in a much better way.

Alvear Avenue *The McGuire, Duhau and Anchorena palaces, witnesses of the 'porteño' belle époque, can be appreciated.*

Alvear Avenue

With its French-style architecture, it is a piece of Paris in the most distinguished area of the Argentine capital. It is hardly 600 meters long stretching from the embankment 'barrancas' of Plaza Francia in the heart of Recoleta up to the the French Embassy mansion, at the end of the 9 de Julio Ave.

The most noted names of the *haute-couture* aristocracy, such as Hermès, Cartier, Louis Vuitton, Ralph Lauren, Armani, Escada, just to mention a few, can be found here. The old seigniorial mansions have been recycled and turned into elegant boutiques, art galleries, five-star hotels, first class jewel stores and luxury residencies.

The Alvear Palace Hotel, inaugurated in 1932 and built in the *Belle Epoque* is located here; as well as the Park Hyatt Buenos Aires that occupies the old Duhau Palace from 1890; the neighboring palace in an Academist style that houses the offices of the Papal Nuncio, close to several foreign embassies such as those of France and Brazil; as well as style is distinguished clubs such as the Jockey Club, a meeting place for the most traditional families of the country.

French Embassy. *It shows the influence of the French architecture in the Río de la Plata area during the 19th Century.*

Elegance. *The interior of the Anchorena Palace.*

Alzaga Unzué Palace. *Currently the Maison of the Four Seasons.*

Recoleta

It is the most aristocratic neighborhood of Buenos Aires and at the same time, a 'must' for anyone spending just one day in the city. The epicenter is Plaza Francia, a quiet embankment 'barrancas' that house a colorful handicraft fair at weekends, which can concentrate over a hundred artisans, besides the street musicians, singers, mimes and multiple spontaneous shows.

A few steps from here, you will see the historical Nuestra Señora del Pilar Basílica, built in 1732, a neighbor of the Recoleta Cemetery where Eva Duarte de Peron's mausoleum is located, among those of other Argentine personalities.

Facing the Cemetery and under the shadow of centenary rubber trees we find an interesting and crowded circuit of restaurants, bars, ice cream stores, movie theaters and discos that are open all night long. The La Biela Café is a classic, with its tables on the sidewalk, ideal to make a pause, ask for a coffee and get distracted while watching people walking by. Also, this neighborhood is a very important cultural icon. The Recoleta Cultural Center is renowned because of its *avant-garde* exhibitions by young artists and at the Palais de Glace – an ice ring and ball room in the early 20th Century when Carlos Gardel used to drop in- where highly interesting artistic exhibitions are now offered. There are also various shopping malls in the area such as the Patio Bullrich, the Buenos Aires Design, devoted to design and decoration and the Village Recoleta, an arcade with bookstores, movie theaters and a fast food patio.

Scenes. Tango school at the Cultural Center and artisans in Plaza Francia.

Recoleta sidewalks. *Enjoying the sunshine at the small tables of the Recoleta cafés steps away from the historical del Pilar Church.*

Patio Bullrich. *Elegant Recoleta shopping centre.*

Alto Palermo. *Large shopping mall located in Palermo.*

Alvear District. *The location chosen by the most prestigious brands.*

Stylish store-window. *A tour to get tempted at every step.*

Rue des Artisans. *One of the alleyways of Buenos Aires.*

Santa Fe Avenue. *To take a stroll and go shopping.*

Old well. *At one of the corners of the Recoleta area.*

Pilar Basílica. *Testimony of the Recoleto monks.*

Recoleta Cemetery. The most aristocratic graveyard of Buenos Aires, with breathtaking mausoleums.

Recoleta Cemetery

Located in one of the oldest areas of Buenos Aires, it is the most aristocratic cemetery of Argentina. In the 18th century, the 'Recoleto' Dominican monks established a convent on this natural slope and little by little the neighboring cemetery continued to grow. Its neuralgic point is the statue of Jesus of the Orchard and from there, the maze-like streets that hide the mausoleums of prominent figures of the Argentine history such as Domingo Faustino Sarmiento, Juan Manuel de Rosas, Facundo Quiroga and Guillermo Brown, as well as Eva Perón.

The cemetery offers an interesting tour among constructions whose styles differ and many of which contain magnificent works of art represented by angels, sculptures, busts and other fine examples of stonework. Guided tours in different languages are offered every day, departing from the entrance of the Cemetery, on Junín 1760.

Works of art. *Most of the cemetery's mausoleums are decorated with sculptures, marbles and bronze.*

Evita's Mausoleum and Monument. *The Duarte Family Mausoleum is the Recoleta Cemetery's most visited.*

Evita's Mausoleum

The Mausoleum of Eva Duarte de Perón (1919-1952), best-known as Evita, is located at the Recoleta Cemetery. Visitors can organize a stroll of the different sites with a map available at the entrance of the cemetery. Anyway, in order to get to the mausoleum where Evita's embalmed body is, you will only need to follow most of the visitors.

Once you enter, by the wall on the Vicente López street side towards the left, you will see the discreet Duarte family mausoleum, with a front of black marble

and a double bronze door, that is always filled with flowers and tourists who come here in order to be photographed beside the mausoleum of one of the strongest popular myths of Argentina.

It is also worth remembering that Evita's body went missing for almost 20 years and that its whereabouts remained unknown until it was repatriated to Argentina in the 1970's. During the intervening years it was buried at the Maggiore Cemetery in Milan. On October 22, 1976, it was deposited in the Duarte family's tomb in Recoleta, which has been its final resting place ever since.

Alongside Juan Domingo Perón. At the Colon Theater.

On the balcony. Evita addresses the crowd in Plaza de Mayo.

Historic. On August 22, 1951, before a crowd, Evita turned down running as candidate for the Vice Presidency of Argentina.

Avenida del Libertador. *One of the most intensively used roads of Buenos Aires, running from Recoleta up to Nuñez.*

Green spaces. *In the area there are various French designed parks, with colorful flowerbeds and antique cast iron street lamps.*

Floralis Generica. Emplaced here in 2002, it is 20 meters high and its petals open as the day goes by.

Avenida del Libertador

One of the most beautiful avenues of Buenos Aires begins in the neighborhood of Retiro, at the bottom of Plaza San Martín and the English Tower and crosses Recoleta, Palermo, Belgrano and Nuñez and keeps going deeper into the province of Buenos Aires, beyond General Paz Avenue. Throughout its course, several beautiful sculptures can be admired, such as those by Auguste Rodin, Emile Antoine Bourdelle and Fernando Botero, among other famous artists.

The 'Floralis Generica', an enormous metal flower with petals that open and close as the day goes by, was emplaced in the area a few years ago.

Also, there are a great number of cafés, ideal to enjoy the sunshine, as well as various museums, shopping centers and first-class restaurants.

Domingo F. Sarmiento. *Sculpture by Auguste Rodin.*

The last centaur. *Work by Antoine Bourdelle, in Recoleta.*

The Sea Nymphs. *Along the Costanera Sur, the famous work created in 1903 by the Argentine artist Lola Mora, can be appreciated.*

Masculine Torso. *Sculpture by the Colombian artist Fernando Botero, located in the Thays Park in the Recoleta area.*

Sculptures

The streets and parks of Buenos Aires are open-sky museums that allow us to walk and enjoy the valuable works of art by noted artists, completely free of charge. The green spots of Recoleta offer an interesting circuit, concentrated in a few blocks. One of the flashiest sculptures is the 'Masculine Torso', by Fernando Botero, located in Thays Park. Two pieces by Emile Antoine Bourdelle, 'Heracles Archer' and 'The last centaur', at the intersection of Avenues Libertador and Pueyrredón, are located a few meters away from Botero's. Rodin's stamp is also present in Buenos Aires streets, the Monument to Sarmiento lies on Avenue Sarmiento and Avenue del Libertador in front of the Planetarium and a replica of the famous 'Thinker' can be seen at the de los Dos Congresos Square, on Hipólito Yrigoyen and Virrey Ceballos.

One of the last pieces that arrived in order to be added to the artistic patrimony of the city is 'Floralis Generica', the gigantic aluminum and steel flower with mobile petals that open slowly as the day goes by, an art piece by the Argentine architect Eduardo Catalano. Another remarkable monument is the controversial 'Las Nereidas' or 'Sea Nymphs Fountain,' a group sculpture by the Argentine artist Lola Mora, made of Carrara marble and pink granite, which is located in Costanera Sur.

Characteristic. Both the dog-walkers and the living sculptures are two 'crafts' that catch the visitors' attention.

Characters

Buenos Aires's charm would not be so if the city did not count on the presence of typical 'porteño' characters, whose colorful touch is a gift for the streets and tours. Some of the nicest are the dog-walkers, young people of both sexes who have found their own 'professions' in walking dogs.

They can be seen while walking along the sidewalks or playing in parks and squares with dozens of animals of a variety of breeds held tight on their leashes.

The hucksters, selling feather dusters, brooms and other assorted objects, are also typical characters of the city, as well as the knife sharpeners who, with their bicycle-operated workshops offer their door-to-door services.

While walking around visitors can also run into talented street musicians, tango dancers who show their class in outdoor "milonga" dances, organ players who are also fortune-tellers and living statues that can stand still for hours...

Outdoor Show. *The streets of Buenos Aires are never boring: colourful feather duster sellers, organ players cum fortune tellers, popular demonstrations, musical bands in the parks, jazz musicians on the pedestrian Florida Street...*

Botanical Garden. *With 5,000 species of plants from all over the planet, it was designed by Carlos Thays over a century ago.*

Japanese Garden. _To travel to the Far East without leaving Buenos Aires. Lakes with fish, Zen gardens and a teahouse in a pagoda._

Gardens in the city

The Botanical Garden, the Zoo Garden and the Japanese Garden are three small oases in the middle of the city. The Botanical Gardens were designed by the French landscape expert Carlos Thays more than a century ago. In it, there are 5,000 plant species from all over the world, grouped by continent that recreate 'small' postcards of different parts of the planet.

The Zoo is just a few meters away, 18 hectares where 3,500 animals of 350 different species coexist in an exotic habitat, with replicas of Hindu palaces, Japanese pagodas and Egyptian temples. White tigers, elephants, giraffes, brown bears and camels stand out.

Much smaller, but equally interesting, is the Japanese Garden, a true Far Eastern corner in the heart of Palermo, with numerous japanese species, water ponds full of multi-colored fishes and a nursery garden devoted to bonsai-growing. Also, there is a nice restaurant-tea house that offers dishes and blends from the distant islands.

From the air. Aerial view of the famous Palermo Rosedal rose garden in which its pure French design can be appreciated.

Parque 3 de Febrero

It is the biggest green lung of Buenos Aires, designed in the late 19th century by the French landscape specialist Carlos Thays and proposed by Domingo Faustino Sarmiento, who was inspired by the Bois de Boulogne in Paris and London's Hyde Park to provide the city with a healthy recreational site. The Park stands out because of its arboreal wealth: jacarandas, acacias,

palm trees and the great historical magnolia, planted by the Argentine President Nicolás Avellaneda in 1875. It is here where the Planetarium is located, with its enigmatic building and shows for audiences of all ages; the Japanese Garden with its pagodas and Zen design and various lakes where boats or water bicycles can be rented in order to have a good time.

It is also the home of El Rosedal rose garden, with a beautiful Andalusian patio and, a few meters away, the

Activities. *The park has a central lake with boats that can be rented and the only golf course in the city.*

Eduardo Sivori Museum that houses a collection of paintings, sculptures, drawings and tapestries from the 19th and 20th Centuries.

The Municipal Golf Course is within the Parque 3 de Febrero: an 18-hole course with lakes and important woods.

The Park is enriched by an important variety of sculptures among which a statue of Domingo Faustino Sarmiento signed by Auguste Rodin stands out, as well as a piece dedicated to Little Red Riding hood, among others. The 3 de Febrero Park is one of the most visited places for training or the classic strolls by the 'porteños' during the weekends, when people enjoy it by foot, on bicycle, by car or on roller skates.

Traditional visit. *Having a tour round Palermo in a horse drawn 'mateo' carriage is an old custom that remains popular to this day.*

Rosedal rose garden. *A beautiful rose garden, with promenades, sculptures and a surprising Andalusian patio.*

Galileo Galilei Planetarium. *To learn about the cosmos and get to know about the enormous meteors found in Argentina.*

Palermo Lakes. *They offer different possibilities: renting boats, riding water bikes, having a stroll around it...*

Farming Exhibition

The annual Rural Exhibition, considered the most important farming event of Latin America, has been taking place for well over a century. Companies connected with the countryside exhibit their novelties and machinery while breeders compete for the top prizes for their animals. They exhibit everything from horses, cows and bulls of different breeds to sheep, pigs, llamas, chickens and rabbits.

Major species are exhibited while parading across the central track, accompanied by their trainers in order to show their beauty and qualities. In the meantime, they are rated by a jury that acts publicly, providing an explanation for each of its decisions. The Grand Champion is the main award, a guarantee of quality and a source of pride that owners will cherish for a lifetime. Once the competition is over, most animals are put up for auction and are sold to the highest bidder.

The central track is the neuralgic point of La Rural, where shows and exhibitions with horses of different breeds also take place.

The Argentine provinces also have their stands in which they exhibit and promote their regional products, fabrics, foods, jams, wines, etc. Food and car companies as well as many brands of rural-style clothing also exhibit their novelties and collections, many times with convenient discount prices.

There are also many restaurants and barbeque "parrillas al paso" that make you sit down in order to enjoy a good 'asado'.

Rural Exhibition. An Argentine tradition that is already 120 years old.

Central track. *The place where the best exhibits of each group are paraded in order to pick out the Grand Champions.*

Regional goods. *Leather handicrafts and homemade delicatessen are two of the specialties people look for the most.*

Palermo Horse Track. *The most important races of the turf calendar are disputed on its main track.*

Palermo Racetrack

It is the epicenter of the horse racing activity in Buenos Aires. It was inaugurated in 1876 and throughout its history it has witnessed the performances of the most outstanding jockeys such as Irineo Leguisamo and Marina Lezcano, besides glorious racing thoroughbreds like Old Man, Botafogo, La Misión and Yatasto, among others. The Palermo Horse Racetrack has three tracks of sand, two are used exclusively for horse training and the main track, one of the best of the world due to its layout is 2,400 meters long and is used for competitions. The Racetrack has three grandstands from where the show can be enjoyed: the Official, Special and Paddock grandstands, besides a nice restaurant with a great view of the main track and the famous Paris Café. The main competitions held here are the Argentine Republic Grand Prize, during the fall and the Grand National Prize, considered the National Derby, that takes place in November.

Argentine Polo Open Tournament. *Palermo field # 1 is known as "the Cathedral of Polo".*

Polo

The Argentine Polo Field of Palermo is the gentlemen's sports cathedral. The premises has two fields, but it is on the Field # one where the Argentine Open Tournament final takes place, where the best eight teams of the world contend.

It is the world's most important polo competition and where the Triple Crown comprising the Hurlingham Club and the Tortugas Country Club Open Tournaments, is held. The Argentine Open is held between the last fortnight of November and early December; with the players leaving their souls on the field in order to be able to the lift the most valuable cup.

Semifinals and above all, the Open final have become a show worth watching, with the attendance of top models, artists, musicians, sportsmen, sheiks, kings, presidents and other personalities who want to watch the world's best polo.

Palermo. A dynamic and colourful neighbourhood, with street fairs, bars with small tables along the sidewalk and informal musicians.

***A neighbourhood without routine.** In the streets of Palermo Viejo there are street musicians, art exhibitions, charity fairs...*

Palermo Viejo

Until a few years ago, this used to be a typical Buenos Aires neighborhood of low houses, grocery stores, inexpensive restaurants and clubs where the neighbors gathered to play cards. At present, it is the trendy neighborhood of Buenos Aires. Serrano Square is the heart of the area, a small square with a small playground and handicraft stalls, a few meters away from the house once inhabited by Jorge Luis Borges during the 1920s. It is surrounded by bars with tables on the sidewalk, ethnic restaurants and clothes, design and decoration stores. On the corner of Costa Rica and Armenia is where the Costa Rica Square is located, a more trendy circuit with wine stores, *avant-garde* theaters, designer centers and small stores selling everything from hand-made soaps to paper.

24-hour bars. *Day or night, the bars of Palermo are always a meeting point for friends.*

Spirit intact. *A neighbourhood of old grocery stores and flea markets that was modernized without losing its identity.*

The new Palermos

Palermo Soho and Palermo Hollywood are part of the new personality of the city. Around Juan B. Justo Avenue, the old houses gave way to TV stations, audiovisual producing companies, trendy restaurants, bars with well attended happy hours, boutique hotels and small stores belonging to the younger designers.

There are also discos with thematic nights and performances and non-commercial theaters whose plays are off the traditional circuit. The last to arrive in Palermo Hollywood are the design hotels, ample rooms with scarce furniture and lots of natural light, usually run by their owners themselves.

In spite of all this modernity, Palermo Hollywood has not lost its neighborhood charm and essence.

The 'porteño' Statue of Liberty. *A small replica of the work by F. Bartholdi can be found in the Barrancas de Belgrano.*

Barrios Porteños

Beyond the traditional 'porteño' neighborhoods, Buenos Aires has many other districts to take into account. From the 'tanguero' neighborhood of Boedo, famous because of corner of San Juan and Boedo, up to the elegant Barrio Parque neighborhood where the rich and famous live, the city has as many streets as personalities. Immigration was key for the development of Buenos Aires that is why it is not strange to find Arab names in Palermo, Korean in Flores, Peruvian in the Abasto, Japanese in Montserrat, Chinese in the Lower Belgrano and Spanish and Italians in every corner. Also, various commercial districts have emerged, where stores selling specific products are grouped. One of the most convenient is the outlets district, along Córdoba Avenue, from Lavalleja St. to Juan B. Justo Ave. It comprises several blocks where outlet and discount stores of the most popular brands of clothes and shoes have concentrated. The leather district is not far away from here; in fact, it is on Scalabrini Ortiz Ave. and Murillo. The neighborhood of Once, is where the textile wholesalers, who also sell retail, are located. Another interesting district is situated on Libertad St. between Bartolome Mitre and Corrientes Ave., where the gold, jewels and watches buy-and-sell stores are grouped. The interior design district is located in Barrio Norte, along Arenales St. from Cerrito up to Montevideo, where there are many furniture and household-object stores.

Lanin Passage. *300 meters of art in the heart of Barracas.*

Barrio Parque. *The place chosen by the "rich & famous".*

Córdoba Avenue Outlets. *Over a kilometre of discounts.*

Las Cañitas. *Modern and vital gastronomic district.*

Costanera Norte. *Fishermen's Club Pier.*

Once. *A neighbourhood with 'wholesale' prices to take into account.*

Mataderos

It is the best place to touch the Creole roots without leaving the Federal Capital. Every Sunday and a few steps away from the Liniers Livestock Market, in the neighborhood of Mataderos, a traditional fair with music, tastes and smells of the Argentine countryside takes place. Artisans deploy their creations in leather, silver, horn, wood and other indigenous materials turned into belts, knives, ponchos, blankets, rings, bracelets and 'mates', among other handicrafts.

At midday, you have a compulsory appointment at the regional food stands that attract visitors with their smells where you can try 'empanada' pastries, 'asado' barbeque, cornmeal 'humita' and 'locro' or the classic 'choripan' sausage sandwich, among other characteristic dishes that you can accompany with delicious desserts such as quince pies 'pasteles de membrillo', 'alfajores de maicena' cookies or latticed 'pasta frola' tarts. Horse competitions take place once the lunch hour is over, with the horseback 'sortija' ring race and traditional horse races. The afternoon is the turn of the folk groups that show all their grace and prowess with the traditional rhythms led by the 'chacarera' and the 'gato'. It is worth visiting the Corrales Museum, with an interesting collection of Creole objects and the paintings by Florencio Molina Campos, and a replica of a rural "pulpería".

The famous Oviedo Café, is located at the corner of Lisandro de la Torre and Av. de los Corrales.

Mataderos Fair. *A good place to get typical countryside handicrafts.*

Tradition. At weekends, the streets off the Mataderos Market become outdoor folk music "peñas."

THIS IS BUENOS AIRES